Contents

Hina Shah

Introduction

With two sticks you can loop and interlock a length of yarn and produce a fabric. This is the essence of the craft called <u>knitting</u>. The skills of knitting were traditionally handed down from mother to daughter; and this is how I was fortunate enough to learn.

In the past, families often devised their own original stitch patterns in the style of the area in which they lived. When we look at their knitting now, it is possible to tell where the wearer was from.

In collections and museums there are examples of very fine and intricate stitch patterns made throughout history. However, knitting really started to grow with the development of the metalwork industry in the 1800s, when needles became more reliable and readily available. Using these improved needles, knitters were able to produce an evenly-knitted fabric with the result that the craft grew rapidly in popularity. At this point, it was mainly men who were the knitters, and it took them six years to become a master knitter!

Don't let this put you off, however; today, knitting is a fashionable and relaxing pastime – it has been called 'yoga for fingers'! Fabulous, exciting yarns are available and it is a great time to take up knitting, with no boundaries to what you can make. Adventurous colours, textures and shapes are commonplace, and there is an upsurge of interest in the craft, so you will be riding on the crest of a wave.

Once you have learnt a few basic techniques you can let your imagination take off and think of many variations, so get going – and have fun!

FUNKY FACT!
The earliest knitted pieces can be dated to around 1200 AD, and were found in Egypt. It is likely people were experimenting with loops of yarn and discovering the strength and versatility of a flexible piece of fabric well before this date.

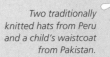

Two traditionally knitted hats from Peru and a child's waistcoat from Pakistan.

Materials

☀ Yarns

There are lots of funky yarns available, including thick, thin, fur, printed, randomly dyed and glitter yarns. It is also possible to knit with wire, string, raffia, plastic bags torn into lengths, fabric and feathers.

   Do not be tempted to use old oddments of yarn that you don't like, because you will not like the finished piece and your enthusiasm will wane. Buying yarns in the colours and textures that you like will ensure that your finished pieces look beautiful, and will give you work of which you can be proud.

❋ Knitting needles

Knitting needles are available in many different materials, including wood, plastic and metal. While wood and bamboo needles are available, I would recommend that you use aluminium needles. These are light and glide through the yarn.

The size of the needle is based on its diameter. As a rough rule, the thicker the yarn, the larger the needle you will need to use.

Make sure that you use smooth, undamaged needles as they will slide through the yarn and help you keep an even <u>tension</u> (see page 11) throughout your work.

Crochet hooks

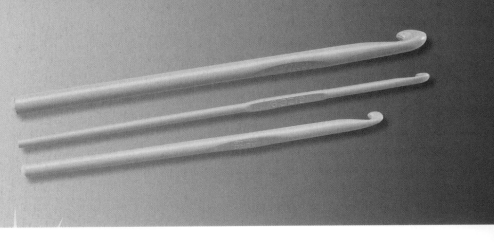

Crochet hooks are very useful for picking up dropped stitches (see pages 22–23) and working edges and fringes. Like knitting needles, they are available in different sizes, and it is a good idea to have a selection.

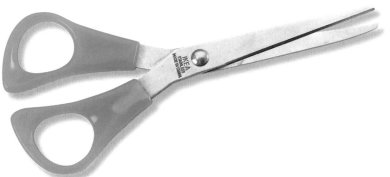

Scissors

Buy a small pair of sharply-pointed scissors. They are used for cutting the yarn and trimming the fringes. Do not use these for cutting paper, as this will make them blunt.

Darning and tapestry needles

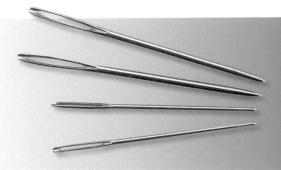

These are larger than regular sewing needles and have a blunt end so that you will not split the yarn when sewing up pieces. There are two main types of needles you will use, so it is a good idea to have both sorts. Darning needles are large, chunky and used for sewing thicker yarns ends. Tapestry needles, also known as ballpoint needles, are smaller and are used for sewing with finer yarn.

Pins

Glass-headed pins in bright colours are ideal, as they are easily spotted when taking them out of your work. They are used for temporarily holding knitted pieces together while you sew them to one another. The longer pins at the right of the picture are quilting pins, and are useful for thicker, chunky yarn.

Row counter

These slide on to the needle and you change the number with each row that you knit, in order to check how far through the pattern you have got.

Tape measure

This is used to measure your work as you knit, and is also used when you check the tension.

 ## Decorations

Collect buttons from charity or second-hand shops and old clothes. They are not only useful as a fastening but also as decorations. Buttons can be found in lots of different textures, sizes and colours; and the wider and more varied your selection, the better.

My personal preference is for natural buttons in wood, shell, horn or stone, as these look wonderful on textured yarn, but glass, plastic and metal buttons are also available in funky colours and shapes. They can be used as a decoration by sewing several shapes and sizes on to bags or scarves.

TOP TIP!

Metal buttons can wear and cut the thread used to secure them. Use waxed dental floss to sew them on.

Beads are also available in a variety of sizes and finishes and are great for decorating your work. Take along a sample of the yarn you intend to use and try to thread the bead on to it, as some yarns will be too thick for the bead to slide on.

What you need to know

✳ Abbreviations

Rather than writing out common terms over and over again, most knitting patterns will use shortened versions. These are listed below to help you out.

Table of abbreviations

alt	alternate
beg	beginning
cm	centimetres
cont.	continue
dec	decrease by working two stitches together (see page 21 for the method)
g	grams
inc	increase by knitting into the front and the back of the same stitch (see page 20 for the method)
in	inches
K	knit
K2tog	knit two stitches together
LH	left hand
no.	number
P	purl
P2tog	purl two stitches together
rem	remaining
rep	repeat
RH	right hand
rs	right side (the outside of the piece; i.e. the part that will be seen)
SS	stockinette stitch
st	stitch
sts	stitches
tog	together
ws	wrong side (the inside of the piece; i.e. the part that won't be seen)
yo	yarn over (see page 18 for the method)
*	Marks the beginning of pattern repeats

✳ Needle sizes

Knitting needles are available in lots of different sizes, from very small to very large. The different size needles have different names in the UK and the US, and the chart opposite shows you what each size of needle is called elsewhere. I recommend that you start with some 3.25mm (US 3), 3.5mm (US 4), 4mm (US 6) and 15mm (US 19) knitting needles.

Crochet hooks also have different names in the UK and the US, and the commonly available sizes range from 2mm (US B) to 10mm (US N).

I recommend that you have at least a 4mm (US G) crochet hook. Having a range of crochet hooks in different sizes is always useful when knitting.

Needle sizes

Metric	US
2mm	0
2.25mm	1
2.75mm	2
3mm	–
3.25mm	3
3.5mm	4
3.75mm	5
4mm	6
4.5mm	7
5mm	8
5.5mm	9
6mm	10
6.5mm	–
7mm	–
7.5mm	–
8mm	11
9mm	13
10mm	15
12.5mm	17
15mm	19
19mm	35
20mm	36

Ball band instructions

Most yarn will have a paper band around it with important information such as what the yarn is made out of (fibre content), the weight of the ball and the colour. There will also be an appropriate tension and needle size to use and washing and ironing recommendations (also referred to as aftercare instructions). There will also be a number called the *dye lot*. Yarn is dyed in lots, and each lot can vary in colour, so it is a good idea to buy all the yarn you need for a project from the same dye lot at the same time.

Yarn weights

Yarn is available in various weights, and the names of these are different in the UK and the US. The table to the right shows you what each yarn weight is called in both the UK and the US.

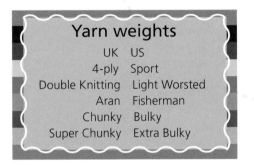

Yarn weights	
UK	US
4-ply	Sport
Double Knitting	Light Worsted
Aran	Fisherman
Chunky	Bulky
Super Chunky	Extra Bulky

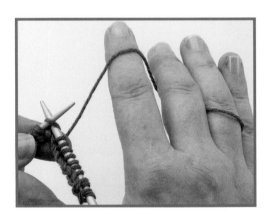

Holding the yarn

There are several ways to hold the yarn, and in time you will find the way that is most comfortable and suits you best.

I prefer to have the yarn threaded over the third finger of my right hand to keep the thread taut as it is being worked. The tension helps you keep your knitting even; and this is essential to keep your knitting looking great. Try different ways of holding the yarn until you find one that is comfortable for you.

Tension

Tension, also known as <u>gauge</u>, is the measurement of the firmness or looseness of the finished piece of knitting, and will tell you how many stitches and how many rows you need to knit to make a certain length of fabric. Normally it is measured over 10cm (4in).

You will find a tension measurement at the beginning of each pattern. To check the tension you will need to knit a square (as shown to the right) slightly larger than 10cm (4in), using the yarn and needles you will use for the project. If it does not match, you will need to adjust the needles you are using. If it is too loose, use smaller needles; if too tight, use larger needles.

It is important to check the tension of each project as it will affect the size of the finished piece.

Techniques

This section will explore some of the simple techniques used in knitting. When you start, sit somewhere comfortable and relax – tense fingers make for tighter knitting, and it is good to have an even texture. Follow the instructions closely and practise the methods until you are comfortable using them.

❋ Slip knot

Before you start knitting, you need to get your yarn on to the needle by making a slip knot. Here is how you do it.

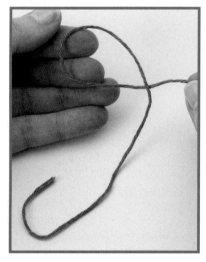

1 Pick up the yarn 15cm (6in) from the end and wind it into a loop by taking the short end over the rest of the yarn.

2 Take the short end of the yarn underneath the loop.

3 Bring the strand up and through the loop, creating a second loop as shown.

4 Gently tighten the first loop, but don't let it close completely.

5 Push a knitting needle through the second loop as shown.

6 Pull the end of the yarn gently to close both loops. This is your first stitch.

Casting on

Your pattern will tell you how many stitches to cast on. There are several ways to cast on, but this is the easiest. Hold the needle with your first stitch in your left hand, and follow the steps shown.

1 Push the right-hand needle through the stitch on the left-hand needle, taking it underneath the left-hand needle.

2 Wrap the yarn from the ball around the right-hand needle.

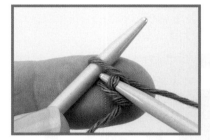

3 Pull the right-hand needle back towards you and catch the wrapped yarn to form a small loop.

4 Lift the right-hand needle up, pulling the small loop of yarn up and out.

5 This loop is your second stitch. Push the left-hand needle into the loop to place it on the left-hand needle.

6 Remove the right-hand needle, then gently pull the yarn to close the stitch. Do not close it too tightly!

7 Push the right-hand needle between the two cast-on stitches.

8 Wrap the yarn over the needle as described in step 2.

9 Pull the yarn through as in step 3.

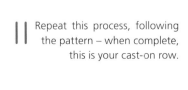

10 Place the yarn on the left-hand needle. This is the third stitch.

11 Repeat this process, following the pattern – when complete, this is your cast-on row.

✳ Garter stitch

The instructions below show you how to make knit stitches. Garter stitch (also called knit stitch) is the easiest stitch to begin with as you knit every stitch on every row. This produces a wonderful, slightly bumpy texture. The knit stitch is abbreviated to a 'K' in patterns.

Knit

1 With your cast-on row, push the point of the right-hand needle through the first stitch as shown.

2 Holding the yarn in your right hand, take it under the right-hand needle.

3 Keeping the yarn taut, bring it between the needles. Keep the needles touching each other.

4 Slide the point of the right-hand needle until only the point is touching the left-hand needle, then pick up the yarn between the needles. This is your stitch.

5 Take the stitch on to the right-hand needle, pulling it off the left-hand needle in the process.

6 You have now worked one stitch and are ready to work the next in the same way.

7 Repeat this technique along the cast-on row, creating a row of knit stitches.

8 Keep knitting along the row. Remember the new row should have as many stitches as you first cast on.

9 Once the new row is all on the right-hand needle, swap the needle to your left hand and continue in the same way.

TOP TIP!
When counting garter stitch rows, each ridge counts as two rows. The other ridges are hidden on the other side of the work.

Stockinette stitch

The instructions below show you how to make <u>purl</u> stitches, which is abbreviated to a 'P' in patterns. While garter stitch is bumpy on both sides, stockinette stitch is smooth on one side and bumpy on the other. To make a stockinette fabric, knit one row, purl the next and repeat. You will soon find the rhythm and it will become clear whether you are on a knit row or a purl row.

Purl

1 Push the right-hand needle into the first stitch of the cast-on row. Keep the point in front of your work.

2 Take the yarn over and loop around the right-hand needle.

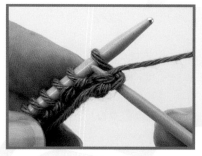

3 Draw the loop through the stitch on to the right-hand needle.

4 Continue drawing the loop through, keeping the yarn at the front of the work.

5 Complete the stitch by slipping it off the left-hand needle and on to the right-hand needle. Repeat steps 1–5 to the end of the row.

TOP TIP!

When the smooth side is facing you, knit the stitches. When the bumpy side is facing you, purl the stitches.

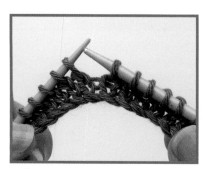

6 Turn the work over and knit the next row, following the knit stitch instructions on the opposite page.

Stockinette stitch has a right and a wrong side, as shown here. Notice the different texture on the left of the picture. This is the 'wrong' side. If you are making a bag in stockinette stitch, make sure the bag is 'right'-side out, and the wrong side is hidden inside.

Moss stitch

Moss stitch is also known as seed stitch, and is made by alternating knit and purl stitches on the same row. It produces a firm, textured reversible fabric, often used as a border on garments.

1 Cast on an even number of stitches, and then knit the first stitch following the instructions on page 14.

2 Bring the loose end of the yarn forward between the needles.

TOP TIP!

There are two main kinds of moss stitch. The example shown here will produce English moss stitch.

3 Purl the next stitch, following the instructions on page 15.

4 Take the yarn back between the needles to the back of the work and knit the next stitch.

5 Knit and purl the stitches alternately to the end of the row. On the return row, start with a purl stitch and then continue alternating between knit and purl stitches.

TOP TIP!

This technique varies depending on the number of cast on stitches. With odd numbers, start each row with a knit stitch, then continue to purl and knit across the row. With even numbers, start every other row with a purl stitch, then knit and purl.

☀ Casting off

When you have knitted your piece of work to the required length, it must be fastened off to prevent it unravelling. Some patterns might refer to casting off as 'finishing off' or 'binding off'; but apart from the names, the method is the same.

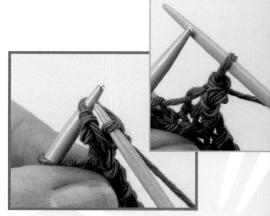

1 Knit two stitches after you have finished the last row. Push the point of the left-hand needle into the first stitch (the right-hand stitch on the right-hand needle, in this picture).

2 Use the left-hand needle to lift this stitch up over the other stitch on the right-hand needle.

3 Let the stitch slide off the left-hand needle (see inset).

4 Knit another stitch and repeat steps 1–3. Repeat this process to the last stitch on the row.

5 Leave the last stitch on the needle. Cut the yarn, leaving a long end.

6 Thread the end through the loop of the last stitch, and pull gently to fasten off. Finally, thread the end through a tapestry needle and sew down the side seam of the work to finish the piece off.

Joining in yarn

If you run out of yarn halfway through a project, or you wish to make items with stripes, you will need to know how to join in yarn.

The process is simple: just cut the old yarn at the end of a row (leave about 15cm [6in] of yarn hanging) and start knitting with the new yarn. When you complete your piece of knitting, thread the spare lengths of yarn on to a tapestry needle and sew them into the edges to neaten the work.

Remember, always join in yarn at the end of a row. Joining in yarn in the middle of a row will leave an ugly bulge.

☀ Yarn over

'Yarn over' is the name given to the process of adding a stitch by wrapping the yarn over the needle. This leaves a small hole in your knitting, which can be used for decorative purposes, as with the leaf pattern (page 32). You can also create a decorative hole in a piece of work by making a yarn over twice and then dropping on the following row, as in the Glitter Scarf (page 26).

TOP TIP!

The technique below is for knit stitches. Between two purl stitches, take the yarn completely around the right-hand needle so that it is at the front. Purl the next stitch.

1 Bring the yarn forward between two knit stitches, taking the yarn under the right-hand needle and then over as shown.

2 Knit the next stitch as normal and then continue.

✳ Decorating tassels with beads

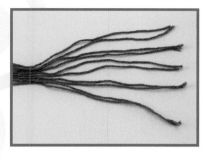

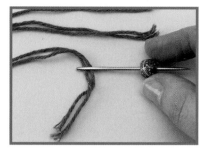

1 Tassels can be made up of a number of paired strands. Separate one pair of strands from the rest.

2 Thread them on to a tapestry needle and put a bead on to the needle.

TOP TIP!

If you want to put more than one bead on the tassels, remember to place the first beads near the knitted piece, and add more beads nearer and nearer the end of the tassel.

3 Pull the bead down the needle and on to the paired strand. Remove the needle from the tassel and tie a simple knot where you want the bead to sit.

4 Repeat this process on the rest of the strands. As you can see, the tassels look great if you thread more than one bead on to each one.

Increasing

Some patterns require you to add extra stitches to shape your work. This is the most common form of increasing, and is abbreviated to M1, which means 'make one' – i.e. an extra stitch is added to the end of the row.

1 Push the right-hand needle into the first stitch of the new row.

2 Knit the first stitch, but do not pull the loop off the left-hand needle.

3 Push the right-hand needle into the back of the same stitch.

4 Bring the yarn forward between the needles.

5 Knit the stitch as normal.

6 Take the stitch off the needle. Knit the next stitch and carry on working. You have now added an extra stitch.

This sample shows how you can gradually expand your piece of knitting by increasing at the beginning of each row.

TOP TIP!

To increase on a purl row, purl the first stitch, then purl into the back, and then the front of the next stitch.

Decreasing

Decreasing is the opposite of increasing. Rather than adding a stitch to shape your work, you take stitches away. The method described below knits two stitches together, decreasing the number of stitches on the row. It is abbreviated to K2tog (knit two together). If two purl stitches are decreased, it is abbreviated to P2tog (purl two together).

1 Push the right-hand needle through two stitches.

2 Bring the yarn forward between the needles.

3 Knit both stitches together.

4 Slip both stitches off the needle.

5 Work the rest of the row as normal.

Similarly to the increasing example opposite, this shows a piece of knitting gradually decreasing in size.

❋ Picking up a dropped stitch in garter stitch

We all make mistakes, but don't panic. A dropped stitch is caused when a stitch falls off the needle and your knitting begins to unloop.

Garter stitch produces a firm fabric and a dropped stitch will generally not run down too far. Regularly counting the stitches on the needle at the end of a row will help you discover if you have dropped a stitch and help prevent them occurring in the first place.

1 Identify the dropped stitch. The stitch above has dropped down to the row beneath the row being worked.

2 Insert the left-hand needle into the dropped stitch, then use the right-hand needle to pick up the larger loop below and in front of the dropped stitch by pushing it through the stitch on the left needle.

3 Ease the loop through the stitch with the tip of the right-hand needle.

4 The dropped stitch will now be on the right-hand needle, as shown.

5 Transfer the stitch back to the left-hand needle and continue your working. Make sure the row looks neat, and continue.

TOP TIP!

Dropped stitches can run down more than one row, creating a ladder effect. If this happens, use a crochet hook to pick it up – see opposite. This is slightly more difficult with garter stitch as you will have to change the direction of the hook on each row.

☀ Picking up a dropped stitch in stockinette stitch

If you drop a stitch when working in stockinette stitch, it can run down and cause a ladder. Don't worry; dropped stitches are easily picked up with a crochet hook. If there is more than one dropped stitch, pick them all up one after another before continuing.

1 Hold your work firmly beneath the dropped stitch to prevent it running down further.

2 Push a crochet hook into the loop of the dropped stitch.

3 Slide the hook through the loop and hook it under the strand of yarn above the stitch.

4 Catch the strand with the hook and pull it through the dropped stitch.

5 Place the stitch back on the left-hand needle.

6 Continue working along the row.

TOP TIP!

If you get a dropped stitch in moss stitch, use a crochet hook to pick up the purl stitch, turn the knitting over and follow the instructions above to repair it.

Rhubarb and Custard Scarf

You will need

1 pair of 15mm (US 19) needles

Three 100g balls of Chunky Print Rowan Yarn: 077 *Girly Pink*

Tape measure

Tapestry or darning needle

Scissors

Card template: 15 x 10cm (6 x 4in)

Crochet hook, at least 4mm (US G)

Tension:

6 sts and 8 rows to 10cm (4in) over pattern

This is a quick and easy scarf to start on, made with wonderful soft and cosy yarn to keep you warm. Wind it several times around your neck and just let it hang down. It is called Rhubarb and Custard as the colours remind me of a lovely pudding my mother used to make.

To make the scarf

With 15mm (US 19) needles and *Girly Pink*, cast on 16 sts.
Knit each row until work measures 190cm (75in). Cast off.
Once you have knitted the scarf, take time to finish your project, as this is just as important as the knitting itself. Sew in any ends following the instructions below. Once the ends are sewn in and secured, follow the instructions on the facing page to add the fringes to your scarf. These fringes are simple to do and are a fun finishing touch.

Sewing in the ends

1 Thread the loose end on to the tapestry needle.

2 Work the needle in and out of the edge of the scarf several times.

3 Pull the needle through so that the end is mostly hidden in the edge stitches of the scarf.

4 Trim away the end of the loose yarn with the pair of scissors.

❊ Making a fringe

1 Wrap 240cm (95in) of yarn tightly around the card template about sixteen times.

2 Cut the yarn on one side only and remove from the template.

3 Divide the cut yarn into as many bunches of four strands as possible. Fold each in half to make a section of fringe.

4 Push the crochet hook through the edge of the scarf and hook a section of fringe at the fold.

5 Pull the fringe through the scarf edge.

6 Hook the fringe further along and pull it through the loop you have made.

7 Keep pulling the cut ends of the yarn gently through the loop, until they are pulled right through.

8 Repeat along the scarf edge, making sure each piece of fringe is attached tightly in the same way.

TOP TIP!

You can make longer or shorter fringes by varying the size of the card template, but the fringes will look best if they are in proportion with the scarf itself – short fringes suit a short scarf.

25

What next?

Now you have finished the Rhubarb and Custard Scarf, why not try making these other scarves? You can make them as long or as short as you like. The first is a stripy scarf that uses the technique for joining in yarn on page 18.
The second variation is a glittery scarf that uses two yarns as one. This gives a different effect and is very simple to do.

You will need

One pair of 5mm (US 8) needles

Two 50g hanks each of Rowan Summer Tweed Yarns: 528 *Brilliant,* 512 *Exotic* and 510 *Bouquet*

Tape measure

Tapestry needle

Scissors

Tension:

16 sts and 23 rows to 10cm (4in) over pattern

Stripy Scarf pattern

With 5mm (US 8) needles and *Brilliant*, cast on 50 sts.
*K4rows stockinette stitch.
Change to *Bouquet*. K4rows.
Change to *Exotic*. K4 rows. Rep. from *, beginning with *Brilliant*.
Continue until the work measures 190cm (75in), ending on the fourth row of a stripe.
Cast off and sew in the ends.

TOP TIP!

Remember that the * symbol means 'repeat from this point', so start from * when you see the 'rep.' instruction.

You will need

One pair of 4mm (US 6) needles

Two 25g balls of Rowan Lurex Shimmer Yarn: 338 *Bedazzled*

One 25g ball of Silk Kid Haze Rowan Yarn: 600 *Dewberry*

Tape measure

Tapestry needle

Scissors

Tension:

12 sts and 8 rows to 10cm (4in) over pattern

Glamorous Glitter Scarf pattern

Using two yarns is as simple as can be. Take a strand of each yarn, lay them alongside each other, and treat them as one strand.
With 4mm (US 6) needles and *Bedazzled* and *Dewberry*, cast on 50 sts.
K1row.
Next row. K1*, yo2, K1, rep.
Next row: K1*, drop the two yarn over stitches, K1, rep.
These three rows form the pattern.
Continue until the work measures 200cm (78in) and cast off.

Two yarns can be used together. The effect you get will depend on the yarns you combine.

From left to right: Rhubarb and Custard Scarf, Stripy Scarf and Glamorous Glitter Scarf.

27

Mermaid's Purse

Make a useful purse to keep treasures or coins in. This basic pattern is so versatile: you could cast on fewer stitches and make one for your music player – or why not knit one to match your favourite outfit?

To make the purse

With 4mm (US 6) needles and *Aqua*, cast on 34 sts.
Knit every row until the work measures 22cm (8½in).
Now K2tog at each end of every row until 12 sts remain. Cast off.
Follow the folding and sewing up instructions below to create the basic purse shape, then follow the other instructions to finish your purse.

TOP TIP!

<u>Oversewing</u> is used to join two knitted pieces together. Fold or place your pieces together and pull a threaded needle up through the edges, a little way in. Repeat along all edges to be joined.

✳ Folding and oversewing

1 Lie the purse flat, then fold the bottom 10cm (4in) up as shown.

2 Thread the yarn from the ball on to the tapestry needle, and oversew the sides.

✳ Attaching the button

1 Fold over the top of the purse and place the button where the middle of the top flap lies. Remove the button and sew a small securing stitch at this point to anchor the thread.

2 Place the button on the purse, and then sew it on to the purse by bringing the needle up through one of the holes of the button and then down the other.

3 Repeat twice more to secure the button, and oversew the thread on the inside of the purse. Trim any excess thread with the scissors.

Making a fastening for the button

1 Anchor the yarn by oversewing it to the top flap of the purse two or three times, slightly to the right of where the button is sitting.

2 Take the yarn over your finger, sew it to the other side of the flap, then bring it back over. Again, sew it to the flap.

3 This forms the basic fastening – so make sure the button fits at this point! Take the needle around both strands of the loop and pull through.

4 Continue around the whole fastening in this manner.

5 When you reach the end of the fastening, oversew several times to secure the loop.

Creating the strap

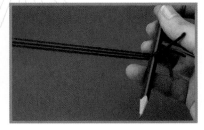

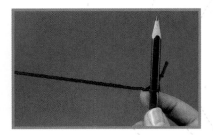

1 Measure and cut three 290cm (114in) lengths of *Gypsy* yarn. Knot the strands of yarn together at both ends.

2 Secure one end of the yarn to a solid object, such as a door handle, and insert the pencil through the free end. Pull the threads taut.

3 Wind the pencil clockwise until the threads kink when you reduce the tension.

4 Hold both ends firmly and release the secured end. Bring both knotted ends together, and hold the middle of the strap to keep it taut. Slowly allow the threads to twist around each other, easing out any knots that form. Remove the pencil and tie the knotted ends together.

5 The strap should look like this once it has finished curling around itself.

6 Oversew to secure the strap to the inside corners of the top of the purse.

The finished Mermaid's Purse.

What next?

Have a go at these alternative patterns for more decorative versions of the basic purse. The first shows you how the different colours make a pretty effect when used together. The second shows you how to create coloured stripes on your purse, and also demonstrates how easy it is to make a bigger version of any of the projects in the book. Once you are happy with the techniques, try making a purse with your own choice of colours for a personalised project!

You will need

One pair of 4mm (US 6) needles

One 50g ball each of Wool Cotton Rowan Yarns: 949 *Aqua*, 910 *Gypsy*, 946 *Elf,* and 933 *Violet*

Tape measure

Tapestry needle

Button

Scissors

Pencil

Tension:

22 sts and 32 rows to 10cm (4in) over pattern

Garter Striped Purse pattern

With 4mm (US 6) needles and *Aqua*, cast on 34 sts.
*K4 rows in *Aqua*, then K4 rows in *Gypsy*, K4 rows *Elf*, K4 rows *Violet*.
Rep. until the work measures 22cm (8½in).
Continue working garter stitch in alternating colour stripes (four rows in each colour stripe), K2tog at each end of every row until 12 sts remain.
Cast off.
Follow the folding and sewing up instructions on page 28 to create the basic purse shape, then follow the instructions on page 29 to finish your purse.

You will need

One pair of 15mm (US 19) needles

One 100g ball each of Biggy Print Rowan Yarns: 237 *Tickle* and 246 *Razzle Dazzle*

Tape measure

Scissors

Tapestry needle

Button

Pencil

Tension:

7 sts and 9 rows to 10cm (4in) over pattern

Chunky Stripy Bag pattern

With 15mm (US 19) needles and *Tickle*, cast on 16 sts.
*Work 2 rows in stockinette stitch (i.e. K1 row, P1 row).
Change to *Razzle Dazzle* and rep. from *.
Continue working stockinette stitch in alternating stripes of colour until the work measures 45cm (17½in).
*K2tog at each end of the row until 1 st remains.
Cut yarn and thread through remaining stitch.
Follow the folding and sewing up instructions on page 28 to create the basic purse shape, then follow the instructions on page 29 to finish your purse.

From left to right: Mermaid's Purse, Garter Striped Purse and a variation of the Mermaid's Purse worked entirely in Aqua yarn.

The top two purses shown with the Chunky Stripy bag (bottom) were made in stockinette stitch instead of garter stitch, and decorated with buttons.

Rosy Bag

This bag is made from strips of knitting and therefore requires very little shaping. Knit all the separate pieces and then assemble them together. Feel free to change the yarns to your favourite colours!

Rosy Bag pattern

Main bag
With 4mm (US 6) needles, cast on 60 sts in *Slosh*.
*Work 4 rows of stockinette stitch in *Slosh*.
Change to *Champion* and work 4 rows in stockinette stitch.
Repeat from * until you have finished 116 rows or the work measures 41cm (16in).
Cast off.

Side panels
With 4mm (US 6) needles, cast on 10 sts in *Champion*.
Work in stockinette stitch until your panel measures 20cm (7¾in).
You will need two side panels, so repeat the above.

Handles
With 4mm (US 6) needles, cast on 80 sts in *Champion*.
Work 4 rows of stockinette stitch. Cast off.
You will need two handles, so repeat the above.

Roses
With 3.25mm (US 3) needles, cast on 12 sts using *Honk*.
Work in stockinette stitch until the work measures 23cm (9in). Cast off.
Following this pattern, make two more roses using *Daydream*, two with *Beetroot* and two with *Wink*.

Leaves
With 3.25mm (US 3) needles, cast on 5 sts using *Splash*.
Row 1: K2 sts, yo, K1, yo, K2 (7 sts on the needle).
Row 2 and all even rows except 14: Purl.
Row 3: K3, yo, K1, yo, K3 (9 sts).
Row 5: K4, yo, K1, yo, K4 (11 sts).
Row 7: K2tog, K7, K2tog (9 sts).
Row 9: K2tog, K5, K2tog (7 sts).
Row 11: K2tog, K3, K2tog (5 sts).
Row 13: K2tog, K1, K2tog (3 sts).
Row 14: P2tog, P1.
Row 15: K2tog; cut the thread, pull through the loop and fasten off.
You will need three leaves, so follow the instruction above twice more.

You will need

One pair of 3.25mm (US 3) needles
One pair of 4mm (US 6) needles
For the bag:
One 50g ball each of Yorkshire tweed DK Rowan yarns: 345 *Slosh* and 346 *Champion*
For the roses and leaves:
One 50g ball each of 4-ply soft Rowan yarns: 374 *Honk*, 378 *Daydream*, 382 *Beetroot*, 377 *Wink* and 373 *Splash*
Tape measure
Scissors
Pins
Tapestry needle
Tension:
Yorkshire tweed DK: 20 sts and 28 to 10cm (4in) over pattern
4-ply soft: 28 sts and 36 rows to 10cm (4in) over pattern

✳ Assembling the bag

1 With the wrong sides (see page 15) of the bag together, pin the first side panel in place on the main bag. Oversew the side panel to the main bag. Repeat with the other side panel.

2 Turn the bag right-side out. Along the top of the bag, measure 6cm (2½in) in from the side along the top of the bag. Thread matching yarn from the ball on to the tapestry needle and oversew two or three times to attach the handle at this point.

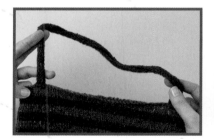

3 Measure 6cm (2½in) in from the other side and repeat the oversewing to secure the first handle.

4 Turn the bag over and repeat steps 2 and 3 for the handle on the other side.

✳ Making the roses

1 Fold the top corner of the strip diagonally until the top corner touches the bottom edge as shown.

2 Fold the bottom right corner in as shown.

3 Roll over three times into a rough tube.

4 Holding the tube firmly, fold the other end of the strip underneath as shown. Continue rolling the rose, keeping the base tight, but letting the top end splay open a little.

5 You will find that this means that the rose will turn until it is horizontal at the fold you made in step 4; and forms a cone shape.

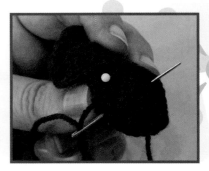

6 Make another fold further along the strip, and continue rolling the rose as before.

7 Continue making right-angled folds and rolling it up until you reach the end of the strip.

8 Thread matching yarn on to a tapestry needle, then put a pin in the base of the rose, and secure it with three or four stitches through the base.

 ## Attaching the roses to the bag

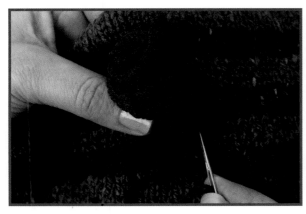

1 Using the same needle and yarn, place the rose on the bag and pass the needle through the front of the bag.

2 From the inside, secure the rose in place with two or three stitches through the base of the rose.

3 Attach the other roses and leaves as shown.

This bag is ideal for holding your knitting!

36

What next?

The roses on the bag can be made individually, so you could just attach them to a safety pin and wear them as a brooch – or you could make some for your friends! They are also great for decorating the other projects in the book. You could add a few to a scarf, or have one as a pendant on a necklace (see the Jazzy Jewellery project on pages 38–39). The bag itself is very versatile. If you want a plain bag, it is simple to leave the roses and leaves off. Here are the instructions for a glittery bag, which is simply an alternative colour version of the Rosy Bag, with slightly different handles and no side panels.

Glitter Bag pattern

Main bag
With 3.25mm (US 3) needles, cast on 59 sts in *Gleam*.
Work 40cm (15¾in) in stockinette stitch.
Cast off.

Handles
With 3.25mm (US 3) needles, cast on 5 sts in *Gleam*.
Work stockinette stitch until the work measures 53cm (21in).
Cast off.
You will need two handles, so repeat the above.

Roses
With 3.25mm (US 3) needles, cast on 12 sts in *Claret*.
Work in stockinette until the strip measures 23cm (9in).
Cast off.
Following this pattern, make two more roses using *Claret*.

Leaves
Follow the instructions on page 32, using *Copper* instead of *Splash*.

Follow the instructions for the Rosy Bag except for the handles, which should be doubled over so they are twice as thick as the previous bag; and sewn on 3cm (1¼in) from the end, rather than 6cm (2½in). In addition, there are no side panels, so fold the main bag in half and oversew the side seams.

You will need

One pair of 3.25mm (US 3) needles

Two 25g balls of Lurex Shimmer Rowan yarn: 336 *Gleam*

One 25g ball each of Lurex Shimmer Rowan yarns: 330 *Claret*, 331 *Copper*

Tape measure

Scissors

Pins and a tapestry needle

Tension:
29 sts and 41 rows to 10cm (4in) over pattern

The finished Glitter Bag.

Jazzy Jewellery

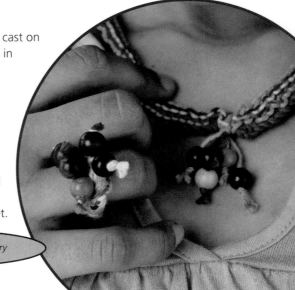

You will need

One pair of 3.25mm (US 3) needles

One 50g ball each of 4-ply cotton Rowan yarns: 129 *Aegean*, 133 *Cheeky*, 137 *Cooking Apple* and 132 *Bloom*

Tapestry needle

Beads (make sure that the tapestry needle will fit through the hole)

Scissors

Tension:

27 sts and 37 rows to 10cm (4in) over pattern

TOP TIP!

Remember, the * symbol means 'repeat from this point'. The knitted-together stitches give shape to the necklace.

Jewellery is exciting to make and these lovely fresh colours will make an eye-catching accessory.

Jazzy Jewellery patterns

Bracelet

Using 3.25mm (US 3) needles, cast on 50 sts using *Aegean* and work in garter stitch.
K1row *Aegean*. Leave a long loose end on each row when you change colours.
K1row *Cheeky*.
K1row *Cooking Apple*.
K1row *Bloom*.
Cast off in *Cooking Apple* and tie ends together.
Thread two of these tied-off ends through the tapestry needle, then thread a bead on to the yarn.
Tie off underneath the bead and trim any excess yarn.

Necklace

Using 3.25mm (US 3) needles, cast on 150 sts using *Cheeky* and work in garter stitch.
K1row *Cheeky*. Leave a long loose end on each row when you change colours.
K1row *Aegean*.
K1row *Bloom*.
*K2tog, K2 sts in *Cooking Apple* and rep. this all across the row.
Cast off in *Aegean*. Trim with beads, as on bracelet.

Ring

Using 3.25mm (US 3) needles, cast on 12 sts using *Aegean* and work in garter stitch.
K1row *Aegean*. Leave a long loose end on each row when you change colours.
K1row *Cheeky*.
K1row *Cooking Apple*.
K1row *Bloom*.
Cast off in *Cooking Apple* and tie ends together.
Trim with beads, as on bracelet.

The finished Jazzy Jewellery

What next?

Why not make some glitter jewellery, which will give a more sophisticated look. Follow the instructions for the Jazzy Jewellery but replace 129 *Aegean* with 338 *Bedazzled*, 132 *Bloom* with 331 *Claret*, 133 *Cheeky* with 330 *Copper* and 137 *Cooking Apple* with 336 *Gleam*. All these colours are from the Lurex Shimmer Rowan yarn range.

Cool Beanie

<table>
<tr><td>

You will need

One pair of 3.75mm (US 5) needles

One pair of 4mm (US 6) needles

One 50g hank each of Summer Tweed Rowan yarns: 528 *Brilliant*, 510 *Bouquet* and 512 *Exotic*

Scissors

Tapestry needle

Tension:

17 sts and 26 rows to 10cm (4in) over pattern

</td></tr>
</table>

Knit one of these cool beanies for every member of your family! The pattern shown here will complement the Stripy Scarf on page 27, but you can play around and use different yarns or embellish the beanie with buttons, badges and beads.

Cool Beanie pattern

Using 3.75mm (US 5) needles, cast on 77 sts using *Brilliant*.
Work 2 rows of stockinette stitch.

Change to 4mm (US 6) needles and work 4 rows of stockinette stitch.
Continue in stockinette stitch and work 4 rows in *Bouquet*.
Continue in stockinette stitch and work 4 rows in *Exotic*.
Continue in stockinette stitch and work 4 rows in *Brilliant*.
Continue working in this order until 36 rows have been completed.
Next row: K1, *K3tog, K6 rep. to last 4, then K3tog, K1 (59 sts remain).
Purl one row.
Next row: K1*, K3tog, K4 rep. to last 2 sts, K2 (43 sts remain).
Purl one row.
Next row: K1*, K3tog, K2 rep. to last 2 sts, K2tog (26 sts remain).
Purl one row.
Next row: K1*, K3tog, K1 rep. to last 2 sts, K2tog (13 sts remain).
Purl one row.
Next row: K1*, K2tog to end of row (7 sts remain).
P1*. P3tog, rep. from * (3 sts remain).

Cut the yarn with the scissors, and then take a threaded tapestry needle through the last 3 sts and sew up the side seams.

Shaping the top

Purl three stitches together, exactly as knitting two stitches together described on page 21, but with three stitches rather than two.

TOP TIP!
To change needles in the middle of the pattern, simply swap one of the old needles for one of the new when you complete a row.

Sewing up

1 Starting from the top on the wrong side, oversew down the seam.

2 Continue all the way down the seam of the beanie.

3 Oversew several times at the bottom, then trim the loose ends.

What next?

Use *Girly Pink* yarn and 15mm (US 19) needles to knit a beanie in garter stitch (see page 14) to go with your Rhubarb and Custard Scarf.

Use *Cheeky* yarn and 6mm (US 10) needles to make a beanie in moss stitch (see page 16), then attach a flower on to the front of it. To make the flower, follow the method on pages 42–43, but use 6mm (US 10) needles and *Swish*.

The finished Cool Beanie

Flower Belt

You will need

One pair of 4mm (US 6) needles

Rowan Denim yarn: One 50g ball of 231 *Tennessee*

Beads

Tape measure

Scissors

Tapestry needle

Crochet hook (at least 4mm)

Tension:

24 sts and 32 rows to 10cm (4in) over pattern

This is a very easy belt to knit, embellished with versatile flowers. Although the flowers may look complicated, take each step slowly and you will be fine.

Flower Belt pattern

Main belt

Using 4mm (US 6) needles, cast on 10 sts using *Tennessee* and knit until the work measures 77cm (30in).
(Alter this length to suit your own hip measurement).
Cast off.

Flowers

Using 4mm (US 6) needles, cast on 68 sts.
Row 1: Purl
Row 2: K2, *K1, place this stitch back on to the left-hand needle, then follow the steps below.

1 Lift stitches one at a time over the third stitch on the row.

2 Continuing lifting stitches until you have lifted eight stitches over the third stitch.

3 Yarn over twice, then knit three more stitches and repeat from * until you reach the end of the row.

Row 2 should look like this when it is completed.

42

Row 3: K1*, P2tog, then follow the steps below.

4 Drop one yarn over.

5 Knit into the front of the yarn over. Do not pull the stitch off the needle yet.

6 Bring the yarn forward and purl into the stitch.

7 Take the yarn back and knit into the front of the yarn over again.

8 Take the yarn forward and purl into the stitch one more time.

9 Drop the yarn over, and then follow the steps below.

Row 3 (cont.): P1, rep. from * to last st. K1.
Knit the next 3 rows. (These three rows can be left out for a smaller flower).
Row 7: K1, K2tog 18 times across the row, K1. This decreases the flower to 20 sts.
Row 8: K1, K2tog 9 times across the row. K1. This decreases the flower to 11 sts.
Cut the yarn leaving a 10cm (4in) end loose, then follow the step below.

10 Thread this loose end on to the tapestry needle, and then push the needle through the remaining stitches and gently pull the flower together. Secure the yarn with three or four stitches and trim with the scissors.

Your flower should look like this when it is finished.

10 Make six more flowers and sew them on with the tapestry needle and some spare yarn, as shown in the picture.

11 Measure five 60cm (24in) lengths of yarn. Fold them in half to make a long tie. Attach to the end of the belt, following the instructions for making a fringe on page 25.

12 Make a second tie and attach to the other end of the belt. Decorate the tie with beads, following the instructions on page 19, to finish off your belt.

The finished Flower Belt.

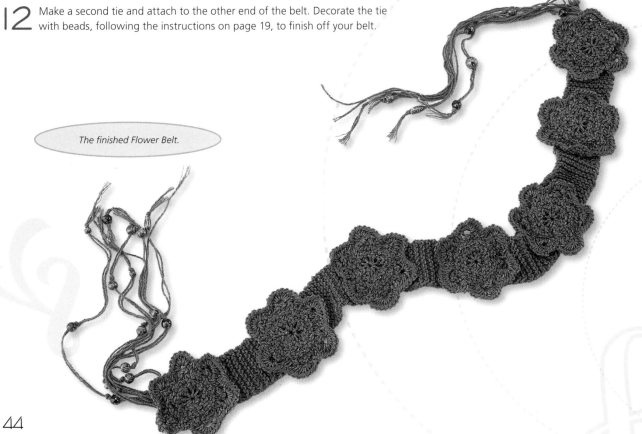

What next?

You can make a simple variation by
changing the colours of the flowers
and the ties.

Big Bag

This roomy bag will be useful
to carry school things, books or
shopping. Make longer handles or
use a variegated yarn for a different look.

Big Bag pattern

Main bag
Using 6mm (US 10) needles, cast on 40 sts using *Cheeky*.
Work moss stitch to the end of the rows:
Row 1: *K1, P1. Repeat from * to the end of the row.
Row 2: *P1, K1. Repeat from * to the end of the row. These two rows make a
moss stitch pattern. Repeat until the work measures 62cm (24½in).
Cast off.

Side panels
Using 6mm (US 10) needles, cast on 5 sts using *Cheeky*.
Work moss stitch until the work measures 30cm (11¾in).
Cast off. You need two side panels, so repeat the pattern for the second one.

Handles
Using 6mm (US 10) needles, cast on 3 sts using *Cheeky*.
Work moss stitch until the work measures 60cm (23½in).
Cast off. You need two handles, so repeat the pattern for the second.

Flowers
Follow the method on pages 42–43 to make the flowers, but use 6mm (US
10) needles. Make four flowers in *Whoosh*, and two in *Cassis*.

Leaves
Follow the method on page 32 to make six leaves, but use 6mm (US 10)
needles and *Swish*.

Making up the bag
Follow the folding and sewing
up instructions below to finish
your bag.

1 Oversew the sides, and attach the
handles 6cm (2¼in) in from each side,
following the instructions on page 33.

2 Turn the bag inside out and
secure the flowers and leaves by
oversewing, as shown.

3 Turn the bag the right way out
and attach the flowers and leaves
on the back as in step 2.

More books to read

Kid's Knitting: Projects for Kids of All Ages by Melanie Falick, Kristin Nicholas and Chris Harlove, Artisan, 2003

Kids Can Knit: Fun and Easy Projects for Small Knitters by Carolyn Clewer, Quarto, 2003

Knitting, Kids Can Do It by Judy Ann Sadler and Esperanca Melo, Kids Can Press, 2002

Glossary

Knitting The interlocking of stitches with a length of yarn with two needles.

Oversewing Joining two pieces of knitting with a length of yarn and a needle.

Purl A type of stitch that helps you to knit decorative fabrics.

Tension or **Gauge** This is the recommended number of stitches and rows to a certain size, given in the pattern. Different tensions can be achieved by altering yarn and needle size.

Yarn over A technique that is used for either increasing or decoration.

Index

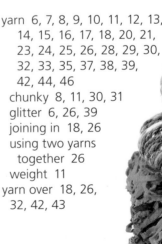